SCHOLASTIC EARLY SCIENCE

Little Flamingo Searches for Food

LEARN ABOUT BIRD BEAKS

Shamim Padamsee

Illustrated by Neetu Sharma

SCHOLASTIC
New York Toronto London Auckland
Sydney New Delhi Hong Kong

As the sun rose over the mudflats, thousands of flamingos stood in the shallow waters, their heads bobbing up and down as they ate.

They were all busy eating. All except Phia, the little flamingo.

'What's wrong, my child? Why aren't you eating?' her mother asked anxiously.

'Oh Mama, why do I have to eat the same food everyday?'

'But that's what we flamingos eat. It makes our feathers nice and pink. Don't you want that?'

'No!' said Phia, stomping her foot. And, with a flap of her big wings, off she flew.

She saw a big banyan tree filled with the chatter of all kinds of birds.

A parakeet was eating figs from another tree.

She watched him open the fruit and eat the juicy pulp.

They looked delicious. Phia tried to open one.

Squish! The pulp splattered all over her. What a mess!

She tried another ...
and another.

SQUISH!
SQUISH!

'This fruit is no good,'
Phia muttered, and off
she flew ...

... to an old, withered tree. She heard a strange tapping sound.

Tap! Tap! Tap!

It was a woodpecker.

'Why are you tapping on the tree?' she asked.

'I am digging for grubs and ants from the bark. They are delicious!'

Phia, too, tapped the tree trunk with her big blunt beak.

THWACK!
THWACK!

'Owww!' Phia screamed. 'That hurts.'

'The ants must taste awful anyway,' she said, rubbing her sore beak, and off she flew ...

... to a tree with lots of pretty flowers—the Red Silk Cotton Tree. A little sunbird was poking her thin long beak into a flower.

Would you like to drink some nectar?' offered the sunbird. 'It is sweet and yummy!'

Phia looked at the little flower and then with a sad voice, said, 'That flower is a little too small for my beak,' and off she flew ...

... to a mango tree. A bird suddenly swooped down with his long tail swirling behind him and caught a fly in mid-air!

'That's quite a neat trick!' said Phia. 'How did you do that?'

'It's quite simple, actually,' replied the bird. 'When you see a fly or an insect, open your beak, swoop down and grab it. Like this,' he said, catching another.

Phia tried but could not shut her beak quickly enough. After several attempts, off she flew ...

... to the ground below. She saw a hoopoe poking the mud with her long, thin beak. 'What are you eating?' asked Phia.

'Creepy-crawlies, of course. They hide under the leaves and stones,' said the hoopoe, swallowing a bug.

How difficult can that be? thought Phia. But when she tried, she could not pick up a single ant. Hungry and disappointed, off she flew ...

... and reached the sea where a pelican was fishing.

'Oh-ho, the pelican's beak is big like mine. If he can do it, so can I!' Phia opened her beak and lowered it into the water. But, when she pulled it out again, all she caught was a long weed!

Phia's stomach was by now growling with hunger. Rumble, rumble, rumble!

Off she flew ...

... further over the sea. 'I am soo-oo hungry,' she said with a sigh. 'I hope I find something to eat soon.'

She saw a cormorant dive into the water and come up a little distance away with a fish in his beak. Phia, too, dived into the water, but ... Pchaak! she fell flat on her belly. 'OUCH! That hurr-rrts.'

She felt awful. The sea-water made her eyes burn.

'Diving is definitely not for me!' she said, and off she flew ...

... to the water's edge, where she carefully watched a heron put her long beak into the water and spear a small crab with it. 'Aha! That looks easy,' Phia said, and put her big heavy beak into the water.

The food tasted delicious. Hungry, she ate and ate and ate until ...

... her feathers became a pretty pink colour. And then, she heard her Mama say, 'Oh Phia, I am so happy you are back! I see that you are eating shellfish, algae and insects again!'

Phia looked up and saw thousands of flamingos standing in the mudflats, their heads bobbing up and down as they ate.

'Oh Mama, this food is the best, after all!' said Phia happily.

FUN FACTS

1. **Flamingos** eat tiny shellfish, algae and worms.
2. They **filter** the food from the muddy water through their sieve-like beaks.
3. Many birds help **scatter** the seeds of the fruits that they eat.
4. Sharp beaks help **woodpeckers** to dig out ants, grub and insects hiding behind the bark of a tree.
5. **Sunbirds** are among the smallest birds in India.
6. Sunbirds help in **pollinating** flowers.
7. The beaks of sunbirds curve downwards to get **nectar** from flowers.
8. Sunbirds eat insects and spiders.
9. Asian Paradise **Fly-catchers** can catch insects on their wings.
10. **Hoopoes** are ground feeders.
11. They have **strong beaks** that can be opened under the ground, and can also upturn stones.
12. **Pelicans** have a pouch under their lower jaw through which they sieve the water, leaving the fish in their beaks.
13. Cormorants have **tooth-edged** beaks to grip the fish with.
14. **Cormorants** can swim long distances under water.
15. **Herons** use their long beaks as spear to catch fish, crabs and prawns.

Shamim Padamsee is an author, educationist, lover of life and nature. She loves writing about different aspects of India – its flora and fauna, arts and crafts and its rich cultural heritage. She runs a website called Young India Books that reviews India-centric books for children. Her motto is Read India. Love India.

Neetu Sharma is an award winning activity and picture book author illustrator. She works with various mediums with ease and has several exhibitions to her name. The detailed appliqué work in her illustrations for *Our Mom is Funny* (Scholastic India, 2013), has been critically acclaimed. This book in plasticine is ample testimony to her dexterity in various mediums.

Published by Scholastic India Pvt. Ltd.
A subsidiary of Scholastic Inc., New York, 10012 (USA).
Publishers since 1920, with international operations in Canada, Australia, New Zealand, the United Kingdom, India, and Hong Kong.

For information regarding permission, write to:
Scholastic India Pvt. Ltd.
A-27, Ground Floor, Bharti Sigma Centre
Infocity -1, Sector 34, Gurgaon 122001 (India)

First edition: December 2013
This edition: September 2022

ISBN-13: 978-81-8477-681-2

Printed at Sterling Graphics Pvt. Ltd., Manesar